Saint Teresa of Avila
for Every Day

Saint Teresa of Avila for Every Day

Reflections from
The Interior Castle

edited by
Kieran Kavanaugh, OCD

Paulist Press
New York/Mahwah, N.J.

The text herein of *The Interior Castle* is adapted from: *Teresa of Avila: The Interior Castle* (Classics of Western Spirituality Series), translated by Kieran Kavanaugh, OCD, Copyright © 1979 by Washington Province of Discalced Carmelite Friars, Inc., published by Paulist Press.

Cover design by Trudi Gershenov
Book design by Lynn Else

Library of Congress Cataloging-in-Publication Data

Teresa, of Avila, Saint.
[Moradas. English. Selections]
Saint Teresa of Avila for every day : reflections from the Interior castle / Kieran Kavanaugh.
   p. cm.
Includes bibliographical references.
ISBN 0-8091-4417-4 (alk. paper)
1. Spiritual life—Meditations. 2. Devotional calendars—Catholic Church. 3. Catholic Church—Prayer-books and devotions—English. I. Kavanaugh, Kieran, 1928- II. Title.
BX2179.T4M6213 2006
242'.2—dc22

                                                   2005037082

Published by Paulist Press
997 Macarthur Boulevard
Mahwah, New Jersey 07430

www.paulistpress.com

Printed and bound in the United States of America

Contents

Introduction

One day when Teresa lamented to her spiritual director that the story she had written of her life was kept (although not condemned) in the custody of the Inquisition, he gave her orders to write another book. In this book she should disguise her identity. Teresa regretted having brought the subject up because nothing could be as difficult, she thought, as writing *another* book. She didn't feel the virtue necessary to carry out the obedience. She experienced in the midst of her struggles with continual sickness and duties of so many kinds a strong aversion toward such a task. But once she began, the work became easier for her; in fact, writing the book brought her much happiness, she said on completing it. Why did it bring her happiness? Because it was a book, like her other books, about *prayer,* and she had many gifts when it came to writing about prayer. The work we now know as *The Interior Castle* has indeed been esteemed by critics as her masterpiece.

Teresa's basic comparison on which she builds her teaching is that of a soul and a castle. The soul of the just person is really like a beautiful castle where the Lord, our King, says He finds His delight. She finds nothing comparable to this castle's magnificent beauty and marvelous capacity. Just as we find it impossible to comprehend God, we can hardly comprehend ourselves because we are made in God's image and likeness.

What Teresa deeply regrets is that we, through our own fault, do not understand ourselves or know who we are. We seldom consider what precious things can be found in our souls or who dwells within them. And so little effort is spent in preserving the beauty of our souls. All our energy is used up on the outer wall of the castle with these bodies of ours. But the fact is that *all* the beauty lies *within* the castle with its many rooms or dwelling places, some up above, some down below, and others to the sides. But what makes the castle so beautiful is the great Light who dwells in the center room and invites us there to enjoy His company. But not only that, as we move through the rooms to the center dwelling place, we experience more and more of this Light which illumines the entire castle for us revealing everywhere its rich treasures.

Teresa is quite sure, right from the beginning, that anyone who does *not* believe in the many favors from God and graces of prayer that are experienced within this castle will *not* experience them. In fact God provides even much more than she can describe. God doesn't like us to put a limit on His works. Unfortunately, there are many who live their lives in the outer courtyard of the castle. They don't care at all about entering and enjoying the wonderful delights that are within. Nor do they have any idea about who dwells within this castle, nor about its resplendent and countless rooms. Teresa compares the many worldly things with which people occupy their lives to vermin, and she says the more they occupy themselves with the vermin the more they become almost like vermin themselves.

So how does one enter the castle? Through prayer and reflection. A prayer in which persons are aware of Christ, the Light, with whom commune and gradually grow in a loving friendship. But there are also many who barely enter the castle. They are very much involved in the world and only once in a while reflect on who they are, usually in a hurried fashion. Their minds are mainly filled with business matters and the world's enjoyments. They need to take upon themselves a life of prayer, and do so seriously. This is what Teresa urges us to do as we follow her on her journey through the castle, through the many lights and darknesses experienced on this path.

When Teresa after many years reached the seventh dwelling place, the Lord then reveals to her something of the favor He has been granting her in the union she has been experiencing. Here the Lord removes something of her blindness and deafness so that she perceives all three Persons in the Blessed Trinity communicating themselves to her, speaking to her, and explaining those words of the Lord in the Gospel, that He and the Father and the Holy Spirit will come to dwell with the soul that loves Him and keeps His commandments. Each day Teresa is more amazed, for these Persons never seem to leave her. Even though the Presence is not perceived so clearly, Teresa finds herself in this company every time she takes notice. But this does not mean that she is so absorbed as to be unoccupied with anything else. On the contrary, she is much more occupied than before with everything pertaining to the service of God. And only when her duties are over does she remain in that enjoyable company.

Teresa, then, not only *knows* but *experiences* God as her ultimate good, beauty, and truth, the source and fountain of all life. She presents God as the most profound lover of each human person, even to those who do not love Him, believe in Him, or even know Him. The most important task in our lives is for us to seek God, find Him, and develop a loving relationship with Him. This leads us to the deepest and most lasting happiness we can experience. These daily reflections taken from Teresa's *The Interior Castle* are meant to help us as we try to carry out this most important task.

January

"Rabbi, who sinned, this man or his parents, that he was born blind?" Jesus answered, "Neither he nor his parents sinned; he was born blind so that God's works might be revealed in him."
—John 9:2–3

1

The strength given by obedience usually lessens the difficulty of things that seem impossible.

2

We now consider our soul to be like a castle made entirely of diamond or very clear crystal, in which there are many rooms, just as in heaven there are many dwelling places.

3

ou should consider what it would mean to this so brilliantly shining and beautiful castle, this pearl from the Orient, this tree of life planted in the very living waters of life—that is, in God—to fall into mortal sin; there's no darkness nor anything more obscure and black.

4

They don't avoid occasions of sin. This failure to avoid the occasions of sin is quite dangerous.

5

I cannot say this without tears and feeling very ashamed that I am writing something for those who can teach me.

6

When it seems they have become lords of the world, at least clearly disillusioned in its regard, His Majesty will try them in some minor matters, and they will go about so disturbed and afflicted that it puzzles me.

7

Since these dwelling places now are close to where the King is, their beauty is great.

8

In all the things so great and wise a God has created, there must be many beneficial secrets.

9

Having seen their perdition they've already begun to approach the castle.

10

It [the soul] rests neither in spiritual delights nor in earthly consolations. Its flight is higher.

11

The soul is now wounded with love and strives for more opportunities to be alone.

12

He makes it desire Him vehemently by certain delicate means the soul itself does not understand. (Nor do I believe I'll be successful in explaining them save to those who have experienced them.)

13

The prioress or confessor to whom they relate their experiences should tell them to pay no attention to such experiences, that these locutions are not essential to the service of God.

14

. . . Majesty, as One who knows our weakness, is enabling the soul through these afflictions and many others to have the courage to be joined with so great a Lord and to take Him for a Spouse.

15

For often when a person is distracted and forgetful of God, His Majesty will awaken it.

16

With the strongest yearnings to die, and thus usually with tears, it begs God to take it from this exile.

17

Suffering over one's sins increases the more one receives from our God.

18

The further a soul advances, the more it is accompanied by the good Jesus.

19

And although I have said "some," there are indeed only a few who fail to enter this dwelling place of which I shall now speak [the fifth].

There are various degrees, and for that reason I say that most enter these places.

20

Even though we can do nothing in this work done by the Lord, we can do much by disposing ourselves so that His Majesty may grant us this favor.

21

It must always be understood that one has to strive to go forward in the service of our Lord and in self-knowledge.

22

Even though He lent us the jewel for our own benefit, He has kept the key to the reliquary and will open it, as something belonging to Him when He desires to show us the contents, and He will take the jewel back when He wants to, as He does.

23

The devil gains much and is extremely pleased to see a soul afflicted and disquieted, for he knows that disturbance impedes it from being totally occupied in loving and praising God.

24

The reason is that since it is getting to know ever more the grandeurs of its God and sees itself so distant and far from enjoying Him, the desire for the Lord increases much more.

25

Since the greatness of God is without limits, His works are too.

26

This secret union takes place in the very interior of the soul, which must be where God Himself is.

27

The first effect is forgetfulness of self, for truly the soul, seemingly, no longer is.

28

The Lord gives the soul great stability and good resolutions not to deviate from His service in anything.

29

The soul of the just person is nothing else but a paradise where the Lord says He finds His delight.

30

You shouldn't want to know anything else than that, although the very sun that gave the soul so much brilliance and beauty is still in the center, the soul is as though it were not there to share in these things.

31

But these persons have received a good deal of mercy in that they sometimes do strive to escape from snakes and poisonous creatures, and they understand that it is good to avoid them.

February

❦

But while he was still far off, his father
saw him and was filled with compassion;
he ran and put his arms around him
and kissed him.
—Luke 15:20

1

O my Lord and my Good, how is it that you
want us to desire so miserable a life, for it isn't
possible to stop wanting and asking you to take
us out of it unless there is hope of losing it for
you.

2

There is no certain rule, as you will have often
heard. For the Lord gives when He desires, as
He desires, and to whom He desires.

3

The water coming from the aqueducts is comparable, in my opinion, to the consolations I mentioned that are drawn from meditation.

4

Like a good shepherd, with a whistle so gentle that even they themselves almost fail to hear it, He makes them recognize His voice and stops them from going so far astray so that they will return to their dwelling place.

5

In exterior matters we are proceeding well so that we will reach what is necessary; but in the practice of the virtues that are necessary for arriving at this point we need very, very much and cannot be careless either in small things or great.

6

By going to confession, reading good books, and hearing sermons, the remedies that a soul, dead in its carelessness and sins and placed in the midst of occasions, can make use of.

7

For since the soul is left with these desires and virtues that were mentioned, it always brings profit to other souls during the time that it continues to live virtuously; and these souls catch fire from its fire.

8

You've already often heard that God espouses souls spiritually. Blessed be His mercy that wants so much to be humbled!

9

It is always so closely joined to His Majesty that from this union comes its fortitude.

10

It feels that it is wounded in the most exquisite way, but it doesn't learn how or by whom it was wounded.

11

One should not proceed in a way that is distressing or disturbing to a soul.

12

It seems that His Majesty from the interior of the soul makes the spark we mentioned increase, for He is moved with compassion in seeing the soul suffer so long a time from its desire.

13

As easily as a huge giant snatches up a straw, this great and powerful Giant of ours carries away the spirit.

14

But since the soul has found this path to be so greatly beneficial, it sees that such a path is leading it along the way to heaven, according to what it reads, hears, and knows about God's commandments.

15

These favors are like those waves of a large river in that they come and go; but the memory these souls have of their sins clings like thick mire.

16

And although some persons put many fears in her, she was still frequently unable to doubt, especially when the Lord said to her: "Do not be afraid. It is I."

17

This Presence bears such extraordinary majesty that it causes the soul extreme fright.

18

The evil of offending God is seen more clearly, because while being in God Himself (I mean, being within Him), we commit great evils.

19

In an instant the experience so binds the faculties that they have no freedom for anything except those things that will make this pain increase.

20

Each one of us has a soul, but since we do not prize souls as is deserved by creatures made in the image of God, we do not understand the deep secrets that lie in them.

21

I can say only that the Lord wishes to reveal for that moment, in a more sublime manner than through any spiritual vision or taste, the glory of heaven.

22

It experiences strange forgetfulness for, as I say, seemingly the soul no longer is or would want to be anything in anything, except when it understands that there can come from itself

something by which the glory and honor of
God may increase even one degree.

23
To beseech Him that we not offend Him is the
greatest security we can have.

24
His Majesty, in saying that the soul is made in
His own image, makes it almost impossible for
us to understand the sublime dignity and beauty
of the soul.

25
The works of a soul in grace, because they proceed from this fount of life in which the soul is
planted like a tree, are most pleasing in the eyes
of both God and man.

26
There is great hope that they will enter further
into the castle.

27
But His Majesty well knows that I can boast
only of His mercy, and since I cannot cease
being what I have been, I have no other remedy
than to approach His mercy.

28

For when a soul is in one continual state, I don't consider it safe, nor do I think it is possible for the spirit of the Lord to be in one fixed state during this exile.

March

❦

*"Those who love me will keep my word,
and my Father will love them,
and we will come to them and
make our home with them."*
—John 14:23

1

In all the things that so great and wise a God has created, there must be many beneficial secrets, and those who understand them do benefit, although I believe that in each little thing created by God there is more than what is understood—even if it is a little ant.

2

When God grants us a favor it is a great help to seek Him within where He is found more easily and in a way more beneficial to us than when sought in creatures.

3

Be brave in begging the Lord to give us His grace in such a way that nothing will be lacking through our own fault; that He will show us the way and strengthen the soul that it may dig until it finds this hidden treasure.

4

It [the silkworm] begins to spin the silk and build the house wherein it will die. I would like to point out here that this house is Christ.

5

True union can very well be reached, with God's help, if we make the effort to obtain it by keeping our wills fixed only on that which is God's will.

6

The soul sees secretly who this Spouse is that she is going to accept.

7

I doubt very much that those persons who sometimes enjoy so truly the things of heaven will live free of earthly trials that come in one way or another.

8

O my powerful God, how sublime are Your secrets, and how different spiritual things are from all that is visible and understandable here below.

9

One thing I advise you: do not think, even if the locutions are from God, that you are better because of them, for He spoke frequently with the Pharisees.

10

If the faculties are so absorbed that we can say they are dead, and likewise the senses, how can a soul know that it understands this secret? I don't know, nor perhaps does any creature but only the Creator.

11

I hold that if His Majesty were to reveal this power to those who go astray in the world as He does to these souls, the former would not dare offend Him; this out of fear, if not out of love.

12

The soul wants to flee people, and it has great envy of those who have lived in deserts. On the other hand, it would want to enter into the midst of the world to try to play a part in getting even one soul to praise God more.

13

Thus it didn't seem to her that anyone's wickedness could equal her own, for she understood that there could be no one else from whom God would have had so much to put up with, and to whom He had granted so many favors.

14

She saw clearly that the vision was a great help toward walking with a habitual remembrance of God.

15

Certainly it's not necessary here to ask how the soul knows without having been told who the Lord is, for it is clearly revealed that He is the Lord of heaven and earth.

16

In this vision it is revealed how all things are seen in God and how He has them all in Himself.

17

This person understood how much more severe the feelings of the soul are than those of the body, and she reflected that such must be the nature of the sufferings of souls in purgatory.

18

Since the greatness of God is without limits, His works are too. Who will finish telling of His mercies and grandeurs?

19

The Lord represented Himself to her, just after she had received communion, in the form of shining splendor, beauty, and majesty, as He was after His resurrection, and told her that now it was time that she consider as her own what belonged to Him, and that He would take care of what was hers.

20

For no earthly thing would the soul fail to do all it can and understands to be for the service of our Lord.

21

His Majesty couldn't grant us a greater favor than to give us a life that would be an imitation of the life His beloved Son lived.

22

It is a shame and unfortunate that through our own fault we don't understand ourselves or know who we are.

23

It should be kept in mind here that the fount, the shining sun that is in the center of the soul, does not lose its beauty and splendor; it is always present in the soul and nothing can take away its loveliness.

24

His mercy and goodness are so bountiful, whereas we are occupied in our pastimes, business affairs, pleasures, and worldly buying and selling.

25

Continue to say this verse and often bear it in mind: *Beatus vir qui timet Dominum* ["Blessed is the one who fears the Lord"].

26

God often desires that His chosen ones feel their wretchedness, and He withdraws his favor a little.

27

The term *consolations,* I think, can be given to those experiences we ourselves acquire through our own meditations and petitions to the Lord—those that proceed from our nature.

28

The experiences that I call spiritual delight in God, which I termed elsewhere the prayer of quiet, are of a very different kind, as those of you who by the mercy of God have experienced will know.

29

And this recollection is a preparation for being able to listen, as is counseled in some books, so that the soul, instead of striving to engage in discourse, strives to remain attentive and aware of what the Lord is working in it.

30

Whether you have little or much, He wants everything for Himself.

31

The Lord Himself will become the reward of this work.

April

❧❦❧

"I am the vine, you are the branches.
Those who abide in me and I in them
will bear much fruit, because apart
from me you can do nothing."
—John 15:5

1

Oh, how desirable is this union with God's will!
Happy the soul that has reached it.

2

Look at the multitude of souls God draws to
Himself by means of one.

3

The soul sees clearly that if it has anything
good, this is given by God and is by no means
its own.

4

This action of love is so powerful that the soul dissolves with desire.

5

What will be the power you leave in the soul that is attached to you, and you to it, through love?

6

The soul was never so awake to the things of God nor did it have such a deep enlightenment and knowledge of His Majesty.

7

Since the soul doesn't have anything with which to pay, it begs for the pity and mercy God has always had toward sinners.

8

She would give a thousand lives—if she had that many—if one soul were to praise you a little more through her.

9

If they don't want to stay long in purgatory, the reason comes from the fact of their not wanting to be away from God—as are those who are in purgatory—rather than from the sufferings undergone there.

10

For even though we already know that God is present in all we do, our nature is such that we neglect to think of this.

11

Thus it's necessary to proceed with caution, wait for the time when these apparitions will bear fruit, and move along little by little looking for the humility they leave in the soul and the fortitude in virtue.

12

Within the palace itself—that is, within God Himself—the abominations, indecent actions, and evil deeds committed by us sinners take place.

13

With the presence of this spiritual pain, I don't believe that physical pain would be felt, little or much.

14

You will understand how important it is for you not to impede your Spouse's spiritual marriage with your souls.

15

Between the spiritual betrothal and the spiritual marriage the difference is as great as that which exists between two who are betrothed and two who can no longer be separated.

16

The desire left in these souls that the will of God be done in them reaches such an extreme that they think everything His Majesty does is good.

17

These favors are meant to fortify our weakness, as I have said here at times, that we may be able to imitate Him in his great sufferings.

18

We know we have souls. But we seldom consider the precious things that can be found in this soul, or who dwells within it, or its high value.

19

In the case of a soul that through its own fault withdraws from this fount and plants itself in a place where the water is black and foul smelling, everything that flows from it is equally wretched and filthy.

20

He calls us to draw near Him. And His voice is so sweet that the poor soul dissolves at not doing immediately what He commands. Thus, as I say, hearing His voice is a greater trial than not hearing it.

21

They spend their time well, practicing works of charity toward their neighbors; and are very balanced in their use of speech and dress and in the governing of their households—those who have them. Certainly, this is a state to be desired. And in my opinion, there is no reason why entrance even into the final dwelling place should be denied these souls.

22

But if he strives for wealth—and after possessing it strives for more and more—however good the intention may be (for he should have a good intention because, as I have said, these are virtuous persons of prayer), he need have no fear of ascending to the dwelling places closest to the King.

23

It is for these reasons sometimes that these tears flow and desires come, and they are furthered by human nature and one's temperament; but finally, as I have said, they end in God regardless of their nature. They are to be esteemed if there is the humility to understand that one is no better because of experiencing these tears and desires, for it cannot be known whether they are all effects of love.

24

These two troughs are filled with water in different ways: with one, the water comes from far away through many aqueducts and the use of much ingenuity; with the other, the source of the water is right there, and that trough fills without any noise.

25

It is a great help to seek Him within, where He is found more easily and in a way more beneficial to us than when sought in creatures, as

St. Augustine says, after having looked for him in many places.

26

There is no need here to use any technique to suspend the mind since all the faculties are asleep in this state—and truly asleep—to the things of the world and to ourselves.

27

Let's be quick to do this work and weave this little cocoon by getting rid of our self-love and self-will.

28

One cannot arrive at the delightful union if the union coming from being resigned to God's will is not very certain.

29

How prepared this Lord is to grant us favors now just as he has granted them in the past!

30

When the soul reaches the stage at which it pays little attention to praise, it pays much less to disapproval; on the contrary, it rejoices in this and finds it a very sweet music.

May

❧

"If you knew the gift of God, and who it is that is saying to you, 'Give me a drink,' you would have asked him, and he would have given you living water."
—John 4:10

1

The Lord also has other ways of awakening the soul; unexpectedly, when it is praying vocally and not thinking of anything interior, it seems a delightful enkindling will come upon it as though a fragrance were suddenly to become so powerful as to spread through all the senses.

2

These words remain in the memory for a very long time, and some are never forgotten, as are those we listen to here on earth.

3

When the soul is in this suspension, the Lord likes to show it some secrets, things about heaven, and imaginative visions.

4

It prefers striving to forget its works, keeping in mind its sins, and placing itself before the mercy of God.

5

It then sees that if it had been able to do something, the power was given by His Majesty. This truth is seen with a clarity that leaves the soul annihilated within itself and with deeper knowledge of God's mercy and grandeur.

6

I wouldn't consider it safe for a soul, however, favored by God, to forget that at one time it saw itself in a miserable state.

7

And since the vision is something definitely understood to be a gift from God (and human effort would not be sufficient to produce this experience), the one who receives it can in no way think it is his own good but a good given through the hand of God.

8

Even though a painter may be a very poor one, a person shouldn't on that account fail to reverence the image he makes if it is a painting of our every Good.

9

Let us love the one who offends us since this great God has not ceased to love us even though we have offended Him very much.

10

The soul sees that it is like a person hanging, who cannot support himself on any earthly thing; nor can it ascend to heaven. On fire with this thirst, it cannot get to the water; and the thirst is not one that is endurable but already at such a point that nothing will take it away.

11

For just as in heaven so, too, in the soul His Majesty must have a room where He dwells alone.

12

One can say no more—insofar as can be understood—than that the soul, I mean the spirit, is made one with God.

13

On the contrary such a soul gains a particular love for its persecutors in such a way that if it sees them in some trial, it feels compassion and would take on any burden to free them from their trial, and eagerly recommends them to God and would rejoice to lose the favors His Majesty grants to it if He would bestow these same gifts on those others so that they wouldn't offend our Lord.

14

We have always seen that those who were closest to Christ our Lord were those with the greatest trials. Let us look at what His glorious Mother suffered as well as the glorious apostles.

15

Let us consider that this castle has, as I said, many dwelling places: some up above, others down below, others to the sides; and in the center and middle is the main dwelling place where the very secret exchanges between God and the soul take place.

16

O souls redeemed by the blood of Jesus Christ!...How is it possible that in realizing these things you don't strive to remove the pitch from this crystal?

17

I don't mean that these appeals and calls are like the ones I shall speak of later on. But they come through words spoken by other good people, or through sermons, or through what is read in good books.

18

Behold the saints who entered this King's chamber, and you will see the difference between them and us.

19

And believe me the whole matter doesn't lie in whether or not you wear the religious habit, but rather in striving to practice the virtues.

20

They would be right if they engaged for a while in making acts of love, praising God, rejoicing in His goodness, that He is who He is, and in desiring His honor and glory.

21

He produced this delight with the greatest peace and quiet and sweetness in the very interior part of ourselves.

22

I believe that if we desire to make room for His Majesty, He will give not only this [gentle drawing inward] but more, and give it to those whom He begins to call to advance further.

23

In loving, if the soul does love, it doesn't understand how or what it is it loves or what it would want. In sum, it is like one who in every respect has died to the world so as to live more completely in God.

24

How transformed the soul is when it comes out of this prayer after having been placed within the greatness of God and so closely joined with Him for a little while—in my opinion the union never lasts for as much as a half hour.

25

The Lord has the power to enrich souls through many paths.

26

We must always ask God in prayer to sustain us, and very often think that if He abandons us, we will soon end in the abyss.

27

God gives no more than can be endured; and His Majesty gives patience first.

28

The soul is moved with a delightful desire to enjoy Him and thereby it is prepared to make intense acts of love and praise of our Lord.

29

Even though it seems that everything is going contrary to what the soul understood, and years go by, the thought remains that God will find other means than those men know of and that in the end, the words will be accomplished; and so they are.

30

I do understand that some truths about the grandeurs of God remain so fixed in this soul, that even if faith were not to tell it who God is and of its obligation to believe that He is God, from that very moment it would adore Him as God.

31

The Crucified, Himself, in consoling her
[Teresa] told her he had given her all the sufferings and trials He had undergone in his Passion
so that she could have them as her own to offer
His Father.

June

"Everyone who drinks of this water will be thirsty again, but those who drink of the water I will give them will never be thirsty. The water that I will give will become in them a spring of water gushing up to eternal life."
—John 4:13–14

1

You will indeed know when this fire is the source of the tears, for they are then more comforting and bring peace, not turbulence.

2

When souls have passed beyond the beginning stages, [they say] it is better for them to deal with things concerning the divinity and flee from corporeal things. Nonetheless, they will not make me admit that such a road is a good one.

3

The vision is seen to be a most wonderful and highly valuable favor. The soul thanks the Lord that He gives the vision without any merits on its part and would not exchange that blessing for any earthly treasure or delight.

4

He used to say that wherever we see a painting of our King we must reverence it. And I see that he is right.

5

It also happens very quickly and ineffably that God will show within Himself a truth that seems to leave in obscurity all those that are in creatures, and one understands very clearly that God alone is Truth, unable to lie.

6

Oh, God, help me! Lord how you afflict your lovers! But everything is small in comparison with what You give them afterward.

7

It is a most generous alms to pray for those who are in mortal sin.

8

The Lord appears in this center of the soul, not in an imaginative vision but in an intellectual one, although more delicate than those mentioned, as He appeared to the apostles without entering through the door when He said to them *pax vobis* ["Peace be with you"].

9

These souls also have a deep interior joy when they are persecuted, with much more peace than that mentioned, and without any hostile feelings toward those who do, or desire to do, them evil.

10

How forgetful this soul, in which the Lord dwells in so particular a way, should be of its own rest, how little it should care for its honor, and how far it should be from wanting esteem in anything!

11

God doesn't like us to put a limit on His works.

12

O Jesus, how sad a thing it is to see a soul separated from this life! How miserable is the state of those poor rooms within the castle!

13

One always gains much through perseverance.

14

It's possible that in dealing with these interior matters I might contradict what I've said elsewhere. That's no surprise since the Lord has given me clearer understanding.

15

But in these rooms of which we're speaking, the Lord, as one who is just or even merciful, does not fail to pay; for He always gives much more than we deserve by giving us consolations far greater than those we find in the comforts and distractions of life.

16

I only wish to inform you that in order to profit by this path and ascend to the dwelling places we desire, the important thing is not to think much, but to love much; and so do that which best stirs you to love.

17

For certainly I see secrets within ourselves that have often caused me to marvel.

18

So that the soul, instead of striving to engage in discourse, strives to remain attentive and aware of what the Lord is working in it.

19

And I would dare say that if the prayer is truly that of union with God, the devil cannot even enter or do any damage.

20

It doesn't wonder as much at what the saints suffered now that it understands through experience how the Lord helps and transforms a soul, for it doesn't recognize itself.

21

This union with God's will is the union I have desired all my life; it is the union I ask the Lord for always and the one that is clearest and safest.

22

Love is never idle, and a failure to grow would be a very bad sign.

23

But I would always choose the path of suffering, if only to imitate our Lord Jesus Christ, if there were no other gain.

24

And the soul is so consoled and happy it wouldn't want to do anything but to always praise His Majesty, and praise Him more for the fact that what He had told it was fulfilled than for the work itself, no matter how important the work is to the soul.

25

Nor did Moses know how to describe all that he saw in the bush, but only what God wished him to describe.

26

It happens that within an instant so many things together are taught him that if he were to work for many years with his imagination and mind in order to systematize them, he wouldn't be able to do so.

27

Let's not think that everything is accomplished through much weeping but set our hands to the task of hard work and virtue.

28

It's necessary that we speak to, think about, and become the companions of those who having had a mortal body accomplished such great feats for God.

29

But let the one to whom His Majesty gives these favors receive them with admiration and praise for Him.

30

The safest way is to want what only God wants. He knows more than we ourselves do, and He loves us.

July

❧

*"Have I been with you all this time,
Philip, and you still do not know me?
Whoever has seen me has seen the Father.
How can you say, 'Show us the Father'?
Do you not believe that I am in the Father
and the Father is in me?"*
—John 14:9–10

1
There should be no desire that others consider
us better than we are.

2
The soul is much more detached from creatures
because it now sees that only the Creator can
console and satisfy it.

3

When He joins the soul to Himself, it doesn't understand anything; for all the faculties are lost.

4

The soul always remains with its God in the center.

5

For not only do they not desire to die, but also they desire to live very many years suffering the greatest trials if through these they can help that the Lord be praised.

6

What cannot be done all at once can be done little by little.

7

You have already heard in some books on prayer that the soul is advised to enter within itself; well, that's the very thing I'm advising.

8

I once heard of a spiritual man who was not surprised at things done by a person in mortal sin, but at what was *not* done.

9

The soul especially keeps in mind how this true Lover never leaves the soul, accompanying and giving it life and being.

10

If, like the young man in the Gospel, we turn our backs and go away sad when the Lord tells us what we must do to be perfect, what do you want His Majesty to do? For He must give the reward in conformity with the love we have for Him.

11

For perfection as well as its reward does not consist in spiritual delights but in greater love and in deeds done with greater justice and truth.

12

I have seen, I think, that the faculties of my soul were occupied and recollected in God while my mind, on the other hand, was distracted.

13

Here, in my opinion, the faculties are not united but absorbed and looking as though in wonder at what they see.

14

What we must do is beg like the needy poor before a rich and great emperor, and then lower our eyes and wait with humility.

15

This union is above all earthly joys, above all delights, above all consolations, and still more than that.

16

And with respect to anyone who says that after he arrived here he always enjoyed rest and delight, I would say that he never arrived.

17

Oh, but there remain some worms, unrecognized until, like those in the story of Jonah (4:6–7) that gnawed away the ivy, they have gnawed away the virtues. This happens through self-love, self-esteem, judging one's neighbors (even though in little things), a lack of charity for them, and not loving them as ourselves.

18

His Majesty knows that I have no other desire, insofar as I can understand myself, but that His name be praised.

19

In sum, there is no remedy in this tempest but to wait for the mercy of God. For at an unexpected time, with one word alone or a chance happening, He so quickly calms the storm that it seems there had not been even as much as a cloud in that soul, and it remains filled with sunlight and much more consolation.

20

One thing very certain is that when the spirit is from God, the soul esteems itself less, the greater the favor granted. And it has more awareness of its sins and is more forgetful of its own gain, and its will and memory are employed more in seeking only the honor of God. Nor does it think about its own profit, and it walks with greater fear lest its will deviate in anything, and with greater certitude that it never deserved any of those favors.

21

In a rapture, believe me, God carries off for Himself the entire soul, and, as to someone who is His own and His spouse, He begins showing it some little part of the kingdom that it has gained by being espoused to Him.

22

I have often thought that just as the sun, while in the sky has such strong rays that, even though it doesn't move from there, the rays promptly reach the earth, so the soul and the spirit, which are one, could be like the sun and its rays.

23

The devil cannot give this experience, because there is so much interior joy in the very intimate part of the soul and so much peace; and all the happiness stirs the soul to the praises of God.

24

Since in meditation the whole effort consists in seeking God and that once God is found, the soul becomes used to seeking Him again through the work of the will, the soul doesn't want to tire itself by working with the intellect.

25

And God is so faithful that He will not allow the devil much leeway with a soul that doesn't aim for anything else than to please His Majesty and spend its life for His honor and glory; He will at once ordain how it may be undeceived.

26

I know a person or two persons—one a man—
to whom the Lord had granted some of these
favors, who were so desirous of serving His
Majesty at their own cost, without these great
delights, and so anxious to suffer that they
complained to our Lord because He bestowed
the favors on them, and if they could decline
receiving these gifts, they would do so.

27

Once I was pondering why our Lord was so
fond of this virtue of humility, and this thought
came to me—in my opinion, not as a result of
reflection but suddenly: It is because God is
supreme Truth; and to be humble is to walk in
truth, for it is a very deep truth that of ourselves
we have nothing good, but only misery and
nothingness.

28

It [the soul] is much more detached from creatures because it now sees that only the Creator
can console and satisfy it.

29

Here all three persons communicate themselves to it [the soul], speak to, and explain those words of the Lord in the Gospel: that He and the Father and the Holy Spirit will come to dwell with the soul that loves Him and keeps His commandments.

30

By some secret aspirations the soul understands clearly that it is God who gives life to our soul.

31

The soul has no more fear of death than it would of a gentle rapture.

August

The young man said to him, "I have kept all these; what do I still lack?" Jesus said to him, "If you wish to be perfect, go, sell your possessions and give the money to the poor, and you will have treasure in heaven; then come, follow me."
—Matthew 19:20–21

1

Fix your eyes on the Crucified Christ and everything will become small for you.

2

Not long ago a very learned man told me that souls who do not practice prayer are like people with paralyzed or crippled bodies; even though they have hands and feet, they cannot give orders to these hands and feet.

3

Only what we ourselves can do in prayer is explained to us; little is explained about what the Lord does in a soul.

4

Our faith is so dead that we desire what we see more than what faith tells us.

5

There is no doubt that if persons persevere in this nakedness and detachment from all worldly things, they will reach their goal.

6

When I read in books about these delights and favors the Lord grants souls that serve Him, I was very much consoled and moved to give great praise to God.

7

The soul is perhaps completely joined with God in the dwelling places very close to the center, while the mind is on the outskirts of the castle suffering from a thousand wild and poisonous beasts, and meriting by this suffering.

8

It is in the effects and deeds following afterward that one discerns the true value of prayer.

9

Leave the soul in God's hands; let Him do whatever He wants with it, with the greatest disinterest about your own benefit as is possible and the greatest resignation to the will of God.

10

Even though they have not experienced these things, very learned men have a certain "I don't know what"; for since God destines them to give light to His Church, He enlightens them that they might acknowledge a truth when presented with it.

11

In some way the sorrow proceeds from the deep pain it feels at seeing that God is offended and little esteemed in this world.

12

Don't think the matter lies in my being so conformed to the will of God that if my father or brother dies I don't feel it, or that if there are trials or sicknesses, I suffer them happily.

13

Our great God wants us to know our own misery and that He is King.

14

The soul sees clearly that another greater Lord than itself governs that castle. And this brings it deep devotion and humility.

15

What are we doing? What is causing us to delay? What is enough to make us, even momentarily, stop looking for this Lord as the bride looked for Him in the streets and in the squares?

16

Three things, especially, are left in the soul to a very sublime degree: knowledge of the grandeur of God, because the more we see in this grandeur, the greater is our understanding; self-knowledge and humility upon seeing that something so low in comparison with the Creator of so many grandeurs dared to offend Him (and neither does the soul dare look up at Him); the third, little esteem of earthly things save for those that can be used for the service of so great a God.

17

To be silent and conceal this great impulse of happiness, when experiencing it, is no small pain. St. Francis must have felt this impulse when the robbers struck him for he ran through the fields crying out and telling the robbers that he was the herald of the great King; and also other saints must feel it who go to deserts to be able to proclaim as St. Francis these praises of their God.

18

When the fire in the will that was mentioned is not enkindled and God's presence is not felt, it is necessary that we seek this presence.

19

One should consider the virtues and who it is who serves our Lord with greater mortification, humility, and purity of conscience; this is the one who will be the holiest.

20

Their desire is to satisfy love, and it is love's nature to serve with deeds in a thousand ways.

21

"Let's leave aside the times when Our Lord is pleased to grant a petition because He wants to and for no other reason."

22

His Majesty gives strength to the one He sees has need of it.

23

In the extreme interior, in some place very deep within itself, the nature of which it doesn't know how to explain, because of a lack of learning, it [the soul] perceives this divine company.

24

The very One who gave peace to the apostles when they were together can give it to the soul. It has occurred to me that this greeting of the Lord's must have amounted to much more than is apparent from its sound. So, too, with the Lord's words to the glorious Magdalene that she go in peace.

25

Their glory lies in being able some way to help the Crucified, especially when they see He is so offended.

26

It is necessary that your foundation consist of more than prayer and contemplation. If you do not strive for the virtues and practice them, you will always be dwarfs.

27

The door of entry to this [interior] castle is prayer and reflection.

28

The things of the soul must always be considered as plentiful, spacious, and large; to do so is not an exaggeration.

29

Enlighten the soul that it may see how all its good is within this castle.

30

Be convinced that where humility is truly present, God will give a peace and conformity—even though He may never give consolations—by which one will walk with greater contentment than will others with their consolations.

31

For in order to know ourselves, it helps a great deal to speak with someone who already knows the world for what it is.

September

"From everyone to whom much has been given, much will be required; and from the one to whom much has been entrusted, even more will be demanded."
—Luke 12:48

1

I wouldn't be surprised if the Lord gave me this headache so that I could understand these things better. For all this turmoil in my head doesn't hinder prayer or what I am saying, but the soul is completely taken up in its quiet, love, desires, and clear knowledge.

2

The first sign for seeing whether or not you have humility is that you do not think you deserve these favors and spiritual delights from the Lord or that you will receive them in your lifetime.

3

It is good to be aware that one is in God's presence and of who God is.

4

At least I think that anyone who refuses to believe that God can do much more or that He has considered, and continues to consider, it good sometimes to communicate favors to His creatures, has indeed closed the door to receiving them.

5

Indeed the soul does no more in this union than does the wax when another impresses a seal on it. The wax doesn't impress the seal on itself; it is only disposed—I mean, by being soft. And even in order to be disposed, it doesn't soften itself but remains still and gives its consent.

6

If you were to understand how important this virtue [love of neighbor] is for us you wouldn't engage in any other study.

7

The Lord asks of us only two things: love of His Majesty and love of our neighbor. These are what we must work for. By observing them with perfection, we do His will and so will be united with Him.

8

Is it true that it [the soul] will know how to explain its experiences? They are indescribable, for they are spiritual afflictions and sufferings that one cannot name. The best remedy (I don't mean for getting rid of them because I don't find any, but so that they may be endured) is to engage in external works of charity and to hope in the mercy of God who never fails those who hope in Him.

9

Oh, human blindness! How long, how long before this dust will be removed from our eyes! Even though among ourselves the dust doesn't seem to be capable of blinding us completely, I see some specks, some tiny pebbles that if we allow them to increase will be enough to do us great harm.

10

Oh, how unfortunate the times and miserable the life in which we now live; happy are they whose good fortune it is to remain apart from the world.

11

You already know that discursive thinking with the intellect is one thing and representing truths to the intellect by means of the memory is another.

12

In heaven we will be surprised to see how different His judgment is from what we can understand here below. May He be praised forever.

13

May He be praised forever, amen. For in lowering Himself to commune with such miserable creatures, He wants to show His greatness.

14

Our Lord grants these favors to the soul because, as to one to whom He is truly betrothed, one who is already determined to do His will in everything, He desires to give it some knowledge of how to do His will and of his grandeurs.

15

He defends these souls in all things; when they are persecuted and criticized, He answers for them as he did for the Magdalene.

16

You may think that as a result the soul will be outside itself and so absorbed that it will be unable to be occupied with anything else. On the contrary, the soul is much more occupied than before with everything pertaining to the service of God; and once its duties are over it, remains with that enjoyable company.

17

For it is very certain that in emptying ourselves of all that is creature and in detaching ourselves from it for the love of God, the same Lord will fill us with Himself.

18

It is true that sometimes these things are forgotten, and the loving desires to enjoy God and leave this exile return, especially when the soul sees how little it serves Him. But soon it turns and looks within itself and at how continually it experiences His presence, and with that it is content and offers His Majesty the desire to live as the most costly offering it can give Him.

19

I have already told you that the calm these souls have interiorly is for the sake of their having much less calm exteriorly and much less desire to have exterior calm.

20

Finally, they enter the first, lower rooms. But so many reptiles get in with them that they are prevented from seeing the beauty of the castle and from calming down; they have done quite a bit just by having entered.

21

Knowing ourselves is something so important that I wouldn't want any relaxation ever in this regard, however high you may have climbed into the heavens. While we are on this earth, nothing is more important to us than humility.

22

If the foundation is on sand, the whole building will fall to the ground.

23

We are fonder of consolations than we are of the cross. Test us, Lord—for You know the truth—so that we may know ourselves.

24

Let us look at our own faults and leave aside those of others, for it is very characteristic of persons with such well-ordered lives to be shocked by everything.

25

All the trials and disturbances come from our not understanding ourselves.

26

Let him do whatever He likes with us, bring us wherever He pleases.

27

The fear it [the soul] used to have of trials it now sees to be tempered. Its faith is more alive; it knows that if it suffers trials for God, His Majesty will give it the grace to suffer them with patience.

28

God so places Himself in the interior of that soul that when it returns to itself, it can in no way doubt that it was in God and God was in it.

29

You answer: "No, my great love and the desire I have that souls be saved are incomparably more important than these sufferings; and the very greatest sorrows that I have suffered and do suffer, after being in the world, are not enough to be considered anything at all in comparison with this love and desire to save souls."

30

And be certain that the more advanced you see you are in love for your neighbor, the more advanced you will be in the love of God, for this love His Majesty has for us is so great that to repay us for our love of neighbor, He will in a thousand ways increase the love we have for Him.

October

"The kingdom of heaven is like treasure hidden in a field, which someone found and hid; and then in his joy he goes and sells all that he has and buys that field."
—Matthew 13:44

1

Even though it is true that these are blessings the Lord gives to whomever He wills, His Majesty would give them all to us if we loved Him as He loves us.

2

In what better way can you, when together, use your tongues than in the praises of God since we have so many reasons for praising Him?

3

As I have said, I don't know the reason, but usually they [those whom God has brought to perfect contemplation] cannot practice discursive reflection. But I say that a person will not be right if he says he does not dwell on these mysteries or often have them in mind, especially when the Catholic Church celebrates them.

4

But even though the presence is not perceived with this very clear light, the soul finds itself in this company every time it takes notice.

5

And thus while Jesus our Lord was once praying for his apostles—I don't remember where—He said that they were one with the Father and with Him, just as Jesus Christ our Lord is in the Father and the Father is in him. I don't know what greater love there can be than this. And all of us are included here.

6

Clearly, Jesus' life was nothing but a continual torment.

7

For then it [the soul] didn't understand the tremendous gain trials bring. Perhaps they were the means by which God brought it to the center, and the company it has gives it much greater strength than ever.

8

So I repeat that it is good, indeed very good, to try to enter first into the room where self-knowledge is dealt with rather than fly off to other rooms.

9

It's an amusing thing that even though we still have a thousand impediments and imperfections and our virtues have hardly begun to grow— and please, God, they might have begun—we are yet not ashamed to seek spiritual delights in prayer or to complain about dryness.

10

Nor is there any reason to desire that everyone follow at once our own path, or to set about teaching the way of the spirit to someone who perhaps doesn't know what such a thing is.

11

Let's not blame the soul for what a weak imagination, human nature, and the devil cause.

12

I really believe that whoever humbles himself and is detached (I mean in *fact* because the detachment and humility must *not* be just in our *thoughts*—for they often deceive us—but completely) will receive the favor of this water from the Lord and many other favors.

13

As its knowledge of God's grandeur grows, it considers itself to be more miserable.

14

I know a person who hadn't learned that God was in all things by presence, power, and essence, and through a favor of this kind that God granted her, she came to believe it.

15

I know the torment a certain soul of my acquaintance suffers and has suffered at seeing our Lord offended. The pain is so unbearable that she desires to die much more than suffer it.

16

If we practice love of neighbor with great perfection, we will have done everything.

17

God doesn't desire anything else than to have those to whom to give. His riches do not lessen when He gives them away.

18

The joy makes a person so forgetful of self and of all things that she doesn't advert to, nor can she speak of, anything other than the praises of God, which proceed from her joy.

19

But I say this person doesn't understand herself, because the soul understands these mysteries in a more perfect manner. The intellect represents them in such a way, and they are so stamped on the memory, that the mere sight of the Lord fallen to the ground in the garden with that frightful sweat is enough to last the intellect not only an hour but many days, while it looks with a simple gaze at who He is and how ungrateful we have been for so much suffering.

20

Great is the mercy He shows in never departing from the soul and in desiring that it perceive Him so manifestly.

21

The words of Jesus Christ, our King and Lord, cannot fail.

22

There is a great detachment from everything and a desire to be always either alone or occupied in something that will benefit some soul.

23

But the soul is fortified by the strength it has from drinking wine in this wine cellar, where its Spouse has brought it and from where He doesn't allow it to leave; and strength flows back to the weak body, just as food placed in the stomach strengthens the head and the whole body.

24

In my opinion we shall never completely know ourselves if we don't strive to know God.

25

By gazing at His grandeur, we get in touch with our own lowliness; by looking at His purity, we shall see our own filth; by pondering His humility, we shall see how far we are from being humble.

26

Embrace the cross your Spouse has carried and understand that this must be your task.

27

Perhaps we could truly learn from the one who shocks us what is most important even though we may surpass Him in external composure and our way of dealing with others.

28

Because it has already experienced spiritual delight from God, it sees that worldly delights are like filth.

29

And I would say that whoever does not receive this certitude [that it was in God and God was in it] does not experience union of the whole soul with God, but union of some faculty, or that she experiences one of the many other kinds of favors God grants souls.

30

I believe that, since our nature is bad, we will not reach perfection in the love of neighbor if that love doesn't rise from love of God as its root.

31

Oh, when the soul returns completely to itself, what bewilderment and how intense its desires to be occupied in God in every kind of way He might want!

November

*"Son, you are always with me,
and all that is mine is yours."*
—Luke 15:31

1

Nor is it possible for the soul to forget that it has received so much from God, so many precious signs of love, for those are living sparks that will enkindle it more in its love for our Lord.

2

It seemed to her, despite the trials she underwent and the business affairs she had to attend to, that the essential part of her soul never moved from that room.

3

But it goes about with much greater fear than before, guarding itself from any small offense against God and with the strongest desires to serve Him.

4

So in this temple of God, in this His dwelling place, He alone and the soul rejoice together in the deepest silence.

5

His food is that in every way possible we draw souls that they may be saved and praise Him always.

6

We should set our eyes on Christ, our Good, and on his saints. There we shall learn true humility, the intellect will be enhanced, as I have said, and self-knowledge will not make one base and cowardly.

7

There's no need for us to be advising Him about what He should give us, for He can rightly tell us that we don't know what we're asking for.

8

I understand this union to be the wine cellar where the Lord wishes to place us when He desires and as He desires. But however great the effort we make to do so, we cannot enter.

9

I am amused sometimes to see certain souls who think when they are at prayer that they would like to be humiliated and publicly insulted for God, and afterward they would hide a tiny fault if they could; or, if they have not committed one, and yet are charged with it—God deliver us!

10

One who was in this affliction heard from the Lord: "Don't be afflicted, either they will praise me or criticize you; and in either case you gain."

11

I hold that one who has advanced further along cannot practice this discursive reflection.

12

Interior things are seen in such a way that one understands with certitude that there is some kind of difference, a difference clearly recognized, between the soul and the spirit.

13

That there are trials and sufferings and that at the same time the soul is in peace is a difficult thing to explain.

14

O Jesus! Who would know the many things there must be in scripture to explain this peace of soul! My God, since you see how important it is for us, grant that Christians will seek it.

15

This [strength to serve] is what I want us to strive for, my Sisters; and let us desire and be occupied in prayer not for the sake of our enjoyment but so as to have this strength to serve.

16

Truly, in all states it's necessary that strength come to us from God. May His Majesty through His mercy give it to us.

17

If you should at times fall, don't become discouraged and stop striving to advance. For even from this fall God will draw out some good.

18

O daughters, how much we shall see if we don't want to have anything more to do with our own lowliness and misery and if we understand that we are unworthy of being servants of a Lord who is so great we cannot comprehend His wonders!

19

When I see souls very earnest in trying to understand the prayer they have and very sullen when they are in it—for it seems they don't dare let their minds move or stir lest a bit of their spiritual delight and devotion be lost—it makes me realize how little they understand of the way by which union is attained.

20

If the soul does not withdraw from its Spouse through a very culpable boldness, He will protect it from the whole world and even from all hell.

21

But let not those who can travel by the road of discursive thought condemn those who cannot, or judge them incapable of enjoying the sublime blessings that lie enclosed in the mysteries of our good, Jesus Christ.

22

There are so many and such delicate things in the interior that it would be boldness on my part to set out to explain them.

23

Even though in those other dwelling places there is much tumult and there are many poisonous creatures and noise is heard, no one enters that center dwelling place and makes the soul leave.

24

For, in the end, people must always live with fear until you give them true peace and bring them there where that peace will be unending.

25

It would indeed be novel to think of having these favors from God through a path other than the one He took and the one followed by all His saints.

26

How miserable this life in which we live! Because elsewhere I have said a great deal about

the harm done to us by our failure to understand well this humility and self-knowledge, I'll
say no more about it here, even though this self-
knowledge is the most important thing for us.

27

What hope can we have of finding rest outside
of ourselves if we cannot be at rest within?

28

Works are what the Lord wants! He desires that
if you see a Sister who is sick to whom you can
bring some relief, you have compassion on her
and not worry about some other devotion.

29

Life is long, and there are in it many trials, and
we need to look at Christ our model, how He
suffered them, and also at His apostles and
saints, so as to bear these trials with perfection.

30

But what will these souls feel on seeing that
they could lack so great a blessing? Seeing this
makes them proceed more carefully and seek to
draw strength from their weakness so as not to
abandon through their own fault any opportu-
nity to please God more.

December

*Again Jesus spoke to them, saying,
"I am the light of the world. Whoever
follows me will never walk in darkness,
but will have the light of life."*
—John 8:12

1

Believe me, Martha and Mary must join together in order to show hospitality to the Lord and have Him always present and not host Him badly by failing to give Him something to eat.

2

I'm literally just like the parrots that are taught to speak; they know no more than what they hear or are shown, and they often repeat it. If the Lord wants me to say something new, His Majesty will provide.

3

Well, believe me, if we don't obtain and have peace inside our own house, we'll not find it outside.

4

If you see a person praised, the Lord wants you to be much happier than if you yourself were being praised.

5

Joy makes a person so forgetful of self and of all things that he doesn't advert to, nor can he speak of anything other than the praises of God which proceed from his joy.

6

I believe I've explained that it is fitting for souls, however spiritual, to take care not to flee from corporeal things to the extent of thinking that even the most sacred humanity causes harm.

7

And since through His grandeurs they have come to a greater knowledge of their own miseries, and their sins become more serious to them, they often go about like the publican not daring to raise their eyes.

8

Even if there were no other trial than to see His Majesty abhorred, that would be an intolerable one.

9

What do you think that abode will be like where a King so powerful, so wise, so pure, so full of all good things takes His delight?

10

May He give me the grace to carry out something of what I tell you.

11

The Lord desires intensely that we love Him and seek His company.

12

If it is Your will, my God, may we die with You, as St. Thomas said; for living without You and with these fears of the possibility of losing You forever is nothing else than dying often. That is why, daughters, I say that the blessedness we must ask for is that of being already secure with the blessed.

13

You must note that hardly any of the light coming from the King's royal chamber reaches these first dwelling places. Even though they are not dark and black, as when the soul is in sin, they nevertheless are in some way darkened so that the soul cannot see the light.

14

Let them trust in the mercy of God and not at all in themselves, and they will see how His Majesty brings them from the dwelling places of one stage to those of another and settles them in a land where these wild animals cannot touch or tire them, but where they themselves will bring all these animals into subjection and scoff at them.

15

But this happiness that comes when the virtues of the Sisters are known is a very good thing; and when we see some fault in them, it is also a very good thing to be sorry and hide the fault as though it were our own.

16

Some quote what the Lord said to his disciples that it was fitting that He go. I can't bear this. I would wager that He didn't say it to his most Blessed Mother, because she was firm in the faith; she knew He was God and man, and even though she loved Him more than they did, she did so with such perfection that His presence was a help rather than a hindrance.

17

And in everything concerning themselves they trust in His mercy.

18

His food is that in every way possible we draw souls that they may be saved and praise Him always.

19

Moreover, the many trials that afterward Mary suffered at the death of the Lord and in the years that she subsequently lived in His absence must have been a terrible torment. You see, she wasn't always in the delight of contemplation at the feet of the Lord.

20

Apart from the fact that by prayer you will be helping greatly, you need not be desiring to benefit the whole world but must concentrate on those who are in your company, and thus your deed will be greater since you are more obliged toward them.

21

This fire of love in you enkindles their souls, and with every other virtue you will be always awakening them. Such service will not be small but very great and very pleasing to the Lord.

22

We shouldn't build castles in the air. The Lord doesn't look so much at the greatness of our works, but at the love with which they are done.

23

If we can journey along a safe and level path, why should we want wings to fly?

24

First, it's clear that something white seems much whiter when next to something black, and vice versa with the black next to the white. The second is that our intellects and wills, dealing in turn now with self now with God, become nobler and better prepared for every good.

25

If a person is to enter the second dwelling places [of the castle], it is important that he strive to give up unnecessary things and business affairs. Each one should do this in conformity with his state in life.

26

And force your will to do the will of your Sisters in everything even though you may lose your rights; forget your own good for their sakes no matter how much resistance your nature puts up; and, when the occasion arises, strive to accept work yourself so as to relieve your neighbor of it.

27

And even if I could gain, I wouldn't want any good save that acquired through Him from whom all blessings come to us. May He be always praised, amen.

28

For the storms, like a wave, pass quickly. And the fair weather returns, because the presence of the Lord they experience makes them soon forget everything.

29

Even though our works are small, they will have the value our love for Him would have merited had they been great.

30

Once you get used to enjoying this castle, you will find rest in all things, even those involving much labor, for you will have the hope of returning to the castle, which no one can take from you.

31

May God our Lord be forever praised and blessed, amen, amen.

Bibliography

Donze, Mary Terese. *Teresa of Avila*. Ramsey, NJ: Paulist Press, 1982.

Medwick, Cathleen. *Teresa of Avila: The Progress of a Soul*. New York: Alfred A. Knopf, 1999.

Teresa of Avila, St. *The Collected Works of St. Teresa of Avila*. Vol. 1: *The Book of Her Life*. Translated by Kieran Kavanaugh and Otilio Rodriguez. Washington, DC: ICS Publications. 1976.

———. *The Interior Castle*. The Classics of Western Spirituality. Translated by Kieran Kavanaugh and Otilio Rodriguez. Mahwah, NJ: Paulist Press, 1979.

———. *The Way of Perfection: Study Edition*. Translated by Kieran Kavanaugh and Otilio

Rodriguez. Prepared by Kieran Kavanaugh. Washington, DC: ICS Publications, 2000.

———. *The Wisdom of Teresa of Avila: Selections from* The Interior Castle. Translated by Kieran Kavanaugh and Otilio Rodriguez. Edited by Stephen J. Connor. Mahwah, NJ: Paulist Press, 1997.